SKYDIVER

SKYDIVER

POEMS FOR MY DAUGHTER

Rosa Glenn Reilly

Dedication

For all those who wove the net that held my daughter
in her last four fragile years. For each person who held
her hand, laughed with her, talked into the night, cooked
for us so we could keep going, donated when the funds
ran low, trusted her to work until her brain finally gave
out, cleared brush from her yard, researched, sent cards
and emails, lit candles, prayed and cursed the darkness.

You know who you are.

"Those who truly inhabit our lives
whose faces, whose gestures
like fine choreography align the air,
whose voices enter that ghostly inner ear
so that we shall hear them ten years
later in an empty room at dusk,
never can their presence be replaced."

- *Edges of Emptiness*
Marge Piercy

CONTENTS

HOSPICE

AFTER

Introduction

When I look at this photograph my face breaks into a smile and the happiness of that afternoon comes rushing back to me. I am 22, a stay at home Mom with a small part time job, amazed at my good fortune to have two such incredible girls by my side. On this day Teresa and Tina had worn themselves out improvising with two curtain rods. There were grand orchestras to conduct from the top of the porch steps, a theatrical fall resulting in a wild limp that needed a cane, a violin to play, a class to call to order and many magic spells to cast on cats, unsuspecting motorists and the bully down the street.

A friend dropped by and caught this moment as we were winding down, still in that space of make-believe, just before the curtain closed to what-will-we-have-for-dinner. The three of us have always shared these overlapping worlds of reality and magic. We could always rely on meeting there even in the worst of times. This was especially true when the world turned on its axis making me grasp for Tina, my youngest, the one sprawled across my lap in this photograph.

In February 2010, Tina, then age 43 and the mother of two sons ages 12 and 14, was diagnosed with a very aggressive Stage 3 breast cancer. This type of cancer is often first discovered in Stage 3 or 4. It is also not unusual for it to bypass other organs and metastasize to the brain first, as it did two years later in 2012.

I would like to say that we used our powerful imaginations and otherworldly magic to create a cure. God knows we tried. But this is not a story about magic that bends to our will. This is a story about life and living and love and all that is sandwiched in between when something awful and real and unimagined arrives at our door. This is about humans doing their awkward, sloppy best and losing who we love anyway.

Tina would tell you that her most life-altering experience was skydiving when she was 27. The moment she dove out of that perfectly good airplane, falling headlong into nothingness and felt the wind hold her firmly and with certainty, she knew she could do anything. All her fears, all her doubts and any misplaced identities inside her, gave way to courage and bravery. For the first time she reached out for a life of her own making. Soon after that came marriage, the birth of her two sons, Gabriel and Jackson, and the unfolding of her new career as a first rate editor and a magnificent poet and prose writer.

I have often seen a window open for women in their forties when our wild, unrealized potential meets unreasonable courage and we can feel the person we were meant to be brushing our fingertips. Tina was in the middle of that awakening when illness arrived. She was older and wiser, skydiving into the rushing wind of her life. She was being herself in a way that was fearless in its honesty, challenging all those around her to risk and embrace their own lives. At the end she soared out of our reach, diving into a new reality where we can still hear her call to grab life by the tail and ride it into a new adventure.

As her death became imminent, Tina thought up something she called "the 100 Vials Project". She asked us to divide her ashes into 100 small vials to be dispersed to friends and family with the instructions to take her on an adventure or to one of our favorite places. She refused to accept that she would stop seeing and feeling the world just because her body was not here.

So far Tina has been to Burning Man in the Black Rock Desert of Nevada, been released off the Charles Bridge in Prague and swam with turtles in the clear, beautiful waters off the Virgin Islands. She has sat at dinner with the Supreme Court Justices, surfed the big waves off the coast of Nicaragua and run in the rural fields and waterways of the Philippines. She has been to Africa, ridden a kayak through the canals of Venice and returned to skydive again along the coast of central California. She has welcomed Spring in rose gardens in the US and Canada and sat as a prop on both a Hollywood movie set and a Broadway musical.

Her spirit remains alive.

It is my hope that you will feel Tina in these pages and also feel those who were privileged to walk this path with her. It is also my hope that you will go out, push the boundaries of your expectations and have an adventure of your own in her name.

Rosa Glenn Reilly

September 2016
Houston, Texas

DIAGNOSIS

Sleight of Hand

my daughters believe in magic
they say they learned it from me

one daughter
has a port sewn under her skin
and wigs she doesn't wear

the other is poor as a church mouse
with few crumbs and no cheese

one daughter
believes her body is fine
and the cancer is not happening

except for the infusions and the pills
she takes those

for luck, she says
and because she likes her doctor

the other helps anyone in need
in a fish and loaves kinda way

she always has just enough
and some left over

one daughter plans what she'll do next summer
skydiving again or getting that
children's book written

because you can't die
if you still have things to do

the other reads the Tarot
makes giant paper mache flowers
in her living room
feeds the homeless vet down the street

one believes that gravity
is just a collective hallucination
and that cat spit
might be the cure for all illness

the other believes
that if you teach a child kindness
and how to find the perfect cereal bowl
at Goodwill
you've prepared them for life

and me?

I believe time bends
to wrap around the moments
we want to remember

and that listening
can travel for miles

I believe that death is only life
turned inside out
like a sweater we took off too quickly
on our way out to play

my daughters believe that magic
is there for the taking

always a breath away
in the turn of a hip
the lift of a hand
reaching for someone we love

maybe
they were listening
after all

Small Talk

the pain lives
under my skin

a micro layer of silt
covering my heart

beating not only in my chest
but inside each capillary

a category 5
coursing through each vein

a rustling
throbbing rush

of flood waters rising
fast moving houses

and cows
and trees

a single arm reaching
for rescue

this wild torrent
released by the most casual

how are you?
I'm so sorry

is there anything I can do?

Women's Hospital Surgical Waiting Room

A pale fire
glows
through the walls
of each tent

snug against
craggy cliffs
stakes set deep

in the slippery
mountain rock

each frost-covered dome
holds one
lone climber

unable to ask
one another
in the sterile quiet
hey, are you afraid?

the storm comes
swiftly

the gale unleashed
climbs
and steals

our thin breath
caught high
in our throats

bravery is always
the price
of admission

a silent crevasse
cracks open

laying in
wait

for a misplaced step
an unsteady hand
a cut too deep
a malignant slip

falling into the
blinding
endless
white

the night is long

and even our
surefooted guides
cannot see
the morning

Tattooed Angel

I can't take my eyes off
his tongue piercing
the small white stainless ball

flashing between words
a small click inside his laughter
a metal tic tac inside his smile

he calls me mom

I look behind me
to see who he's talking to

he grabs me up
into his muscled arms
my right ear suddenly tight
against his chest

and then
I hear it

the *boom boom boom*
of his orphan heart

and my shoulders soften

I want to escape
his words

don't worry mama I'll
take good care of her

my mind spins
trying to be still

my tears
crack the cool
surface of his AC/DC t-shirt

an eager puppy
sincere as apple pie
too loud
too talky

man-boy eyes
looking into mine

tangling in my cautious
mother antennae

*don't worry mama I'll
take good care of her*

I look past biceps
lined in purple ink
past the red swirls
and yellow flowers

and see

bags of trash
he has carried to the curb

prescription bottles in a careful line

pills he has cupped in his hand
every four hours
day and night
for her to swallow

containers of bloody fluids
he has measured
emptying her surgical drains

my daughter's
oozing wounds
where only
three days ago
her sweet breast lay

the way he kisses
her swollen hand
with the IV port still embedded

don't worry mama I'll
take good care of her

I look around
the bathroom is clean
the dishes are washed

but he is still
the stranger I met
only last week

the one who moved 350 miles
to join his life to hers

only last week
she was
that voracious woman
bold and sexy

unstoppable

7 days ago
7 centuries ago

and I see it now
in her eyes

when she wakes at night
and he is there

she is that woman
still

because he refuses
to see her

any other way

Memorizing

I have just spent a lazy
sunlit afternoon
in the tender folds of a warm breeze
still holding a hint of Texas winter
teasing
making us believe
we'll have a spring this year

I have spent this afternoon
memorizing my daughter's profile
the lines of her nose
obedient to our latin lineage
distinct for the proud dismissal
of pug or pert
choosing instead a royal touch
of fine bone

I have just spent a lazy
sunlit afternoon
finding excuses to touch
her unruly hair
descendent of nothing
except her own wild contrary nature
answering to no one
disdainful of brush or comb

strands of gold and brown and auburn
a wave here
a curl there
a stray lock of almost gray
like a visitor
dropped off
at the wrong address

as the day turns toward night
we nap
curled
twin embryos
facing one another
only our hands touching
intertwined
as if in prayer

she
exhausted from radiation

me
worn thin from holding
my breath

Dear God

my daughter doesn't believe in you

she doesn't need you
   to make her behave
   or be kind
   to remind her
   not to kill or steal

she doesn't see you as Santa in the sky

receiving the long daily lists
   please give me this
   please fix that

she doesn't blame you
   hold you responsible
   beg for your mercy
   vie for your favor

she thinks the threat of hell is a bit excessive
   high theater
   a little dramatic
   over the top
   only good for inspiring Goya and Dante

someday, she says
she will happily sit down
at the pearly gates
for a get-to-know-you chat
   share a few laughs
   about marketing
   and how you need a better publicist

but for now
   finding you

doesn't touch
waking up from a nap
and finding
her 16 year old quietly stretched out
beside her
his hand softly brushing
the military fuzz of her new hair

it doesn't touch
the possibility of
two more birthdays
and a graduation

so don't wait for her
she's busy

Hobby Airport 7pm

I see them everywhere. The bald heads.
One of them is waiting for a plane to Denver
from Houston. An airport porter pushes her
wheelchair while she balances a carry-on in
her lap. Long limbs, mid-thirties, a black knit
cap on her head and a green jersey hoodie
even though it's July. Her arms are too thin to
stay warm. Another one stands at the ticket
counter, her blond wig askew. She looks away
and doesn't look back. She is still able to walk,
to stand in line. Maybe she's thinking, *that's
not me. I'm not that bad.*

I wonder how many other mothers are
watching these women while waiting for our
flights. Silently. Not knowing one another.
Not able to extend a hand, a small nod. Not
able to quietly lock eyes while the dry terror
creeps into our throats on clawed feet. How
many of us can hear the predator's nails
clicking on the polished floor, advancing
while we grip our coffee cups, our purses,
our laptops, our cell phones. When there is
nothing for us to hold but air.

Pulling Vines

two months out of radiation

I find you
careless in the poison ivy

sticky burrs and wild sage
your stiff grey canvas gloves reaching
high above your head

hands wrapped firmly
around a fistful
of bark-covered grape vines

your still-strong body
leaning
suspended
for a moment

before the give

the let go

the surrendering tear

sending ass to the ground
limbs set free

laughing
from the dark sunless grip

forearm across your brow
palms dusted down your jeans

eyes narrowed
scouring your yard for the next
break out

meditation
in release

exorcism

a garlic necklace against
this smothering
spreading
parasitic death

you are
the avenger
the hero doctor

the shaman
dirt-streaked
and whole

ripping down danger

making room for life

Dreaming Still

dark curls hang damp
against your neck
soft wet life
resting so innocently

today
sweat soaked and happy
we have coerced
threatened and cajoled
the hard packed dirt

digging out stones
clearing the way
for tomatoes
and salt shakers

dreaming of warm, juicy, red flesh
taunting death with another season

dark curls hang damp
against your neck
as we remember
each garden

you at age 4 not understanding
that pulling the small shoots
did not make them grow faster

at 6 claiming your own plants
so you could sell the big ones
to the neighbors

at 13 pretending you didn't care
then I'd find you in the late afternoon
turning the compost

You want to plan next year's garden
you say
maybe add some peppers and spinach

I reach to touch
your damp cheek
and remember

your young baby neck
smelling of milk
now smelling of sweat and clover

and maybe carrots, I say

Beautiful

The three of us sit on the patio
legs resting on chair arms and tables
as the bright autumn moon
races through clouds

darkness hides
my still muted panic
in our warm
familiar gestures

a wash of light across a cheek
a brow
a feathered lash
that we, a mother
and two daughters
have studied in one another
for 46 years

the cats are inside
masters of the house
owners now
of the claw-tattered armchair
and leftover chicken

your hair has grown out
in a Winona Ryder / Kira Knightly
close-shorn crop
and your sister
never one for effusive
sisterly compliments
tells you

you look beautiful

your eyebrows rise in disbelief
head cocked to get the joke

no she says *really*
it's true
you look adorable

and for a moment your scarred
battle-worn body smiles
deliciously young
un-cancered
free of pills and infusions
nausea and tiredness

the damned
weary tiredness

I rise in the moonlight
to place my cheek
against your warm head

I close my eyes
and the fuzzy perfect roundness
brings you again into my arms
small and new

and we start over

side stepping
needles and scalpels
drugs that scorch
the tender flesh of life

soft dark cowlicks
cover your head
growing in this direction
and that

searching
like spirals of fine thread
winding through this labyrinth

marking a path
leading the lost
home again

Anthem

flowered panties
hanging on the clothesline

fluttering lilacs
heaving pansies

undulating sunflowers
in the sunshine

irrepressibly billowing
against the blue sky

a naughty Tibetan prayer flag
announcing

I had sex
with my boyfriend last night

Fuck you, cancer!

I'm still here!

METASTASIS

Apocalypse

yesterday she could not write her name
woke up
tried to pay a bill
couldn't write

so today I am researching
brain metastasis
and 30 screens later
I buy a solar oven

3 months ago
the doctors told her
she was
cured

they keep selling us that word

on billboards
in double page ads
what happened to *remission?*

I feel the rage
of splintered hope
and the next time I go shopping

I carry home a 50 lb bag
of long grain white rice

I read online
this cancer usually spreads
to the brain first

so I order

10 boxes of white candles
20 lbs of pinto beans
rechargeable batteries
and a field guide to edible wild plants
in the city

the brain MRI comes back
showing 3 tumors
one large
2 smaller
14 tiny white tumor seeds
ready to sprout

10 charcoal filters to make dirty water clean
1 snake bite kit
3 machetes
1 pick
2 shovels
and a fire starter

today she has double vision
a black eye patch
and a slight drag in
her left leg
the doctors say maybe a year

I look in my closet
at the shelves crowded with
jars of peanut butter
bug spray
an inflatable raft
bandages

and disinfectant
more supplies arriving
every day

and I know
I will never be prepared

the storm is already here

The Alamo

in Bismarck, North Dakota
and Bangor, Maine
in Columbus, Ohio
a tenement in Rome
the village of Qualida in Morocco
and here, in Texas

how many times each day
are the words spoken?

the cancer has metastasized

to the lungs
to the liver
the bones
the brain

to the brain

the last garrison
the alamo
the last stand

she was supposed to have years
of careful chemo volleys
across crumbling stone walls
waiting for reinforcements

organs invaded and rescued
then hope
and breathing
and graduations and birthdays
and thanks-giving

lots of thanks-giving
before the next battle

but today
the dust rises
announcing
the advancing enemy

and I want to rain
thunderbolts
of mother fury
onto this stained
and worn story

I feel robbed

unprepared for this final siege
to come so quickly

the soldiers scaling the walls
in the hot Texas night
we are outnumbered
outgunned

what happened to the proper order of things?

what happened to the brain always being last?

maybe if I had breast fed her

Trying to Distract Myself while Waiting for Your Next Brain MRI 30 Days From Now

magnetic resonance imaging
mandatory regulated investigation
murky radio-telegraph indicator

messenger related idioms
melodious radical inflections
mellow rueful indifference

metallic R&B inspirations
melodies repeatedly interrupted
monologue randomly interjected

multiplication

no, not that

monsoon rapidly irrigating
moonstruck rain imperative
mediterrean rash initiative

medusa ragefully incensed
midas regretfully ignorant
michelangelo riotously impatient

morphology
meticulous
morphine

ritual
rhetorical

revolt
revolution

iambic

your next MRI

microscopic ripcord imploding

Masks

I only feel sane
when I am with her

this daughter
who carries a constellation
of tumors behind her dark
dancing eyes
in the recesses of cranial folds

the same grey valleys
that hold her love
of editing
her irreverent humor
her full house of memories

the Christmas her youngest boy
made macaroni photo frames
and pitched a shutout
four summers later

the golden fall morning
her eldest brought
his first real girlfriend
to family breakfast
at the Yale Street Cafe

today I bring
organic strawberries from Costco
blueberries
wild salmon
and agave

I clear out the hidden teflon
and plastics
from her kitchen
the packaged foods
with sodium benzoate
monsodium glutamate
nitrates
and colors made in labs
by workers
wearing masks
who wash before going home

she shaves her head once more
hangs her radiation mask on the wall

a metal trophy signifying the end
of a run
a 26-day marathon
of zaps and pings
darting blue lines
that no one can see but her

this is my child

pinned behind that metal grill
mask molded to the contours
of her beautiful face
screwed down to the stainless table

while technicians push buttons
and cower behind
their leaden walls

she sleeps now
one cat covering her bald head
another at the crook of her knee

I linger
after cooking stir fry
orange peppers and broccoli
scallions and tofu

groceries shelved
dishes washed
new grocery list made

I stand above her smiling sleep
kiss her warm cheek
the black marker targets still showing
on her pale smooth head
where hair may never grow

I know the night will nestle
one of her boys
to her side
needing to be close to a mother
in danger of leaving too soon

the morning may bring
enough rest
to work a few hours

I go down the stairs
and get into my car
the mask settling onto the
contours of my own face

re-entering a world that lives
the distance to the moon

away from my heart

Headscarf

Paisley
cotton gauze
pink, orange and teal

tied in a flourish
behind one ear

trails of color falling
over the soft lines
of your shoulder

winter blue
summer yellow
pulled down
just above your brows

and then the black eye patch
the final touch
defeating your double vision

you are ready to face the world
with an *arrrgh*
and a *hey matey*

a turn of your hand
holds the seer's globe
illuminating the mystery

will you walk the plank today
or escape like a mist
into the next caravan headed north

to dance another night
by the fire?

Sudoku

we're talking while I'm clearing the table
loading the dishwasher

you helped me cook
but I do this part faster
so I've taken over

has Gabe heard back from Lewis & Clark?
what did Jack's teacher want to meet about?

how are you feeling after the last infusion?
and that sore on your head?
is it still oozing?

should we put some more of that hippie
ointment on it?
did it help?

your answers float over to me
as I move from dining table
to kitchen and back again.

no. but St John's College is interested.
she said he's brilliant and needs more sleep

ok
yes
yes

then nothing

silence.

I look around the corner
past the living room
and see you through the glass
of the patio door

wrapped
in the soft, thick, beige coat
I helped the boys' father
pick out for you in Chicago

when your hands stayed blue
from late October to May

you are wearing my red knit cap
over your new short, curly hair
pencil in hand
hunched over Sudoku

the rules are simple
each line has nine numbers
each of nine squares has nine numbers

nine is the number of completion

the ones you can see
tease
narrow the options
make your brain reach
for the possible right choice
the only right choice

against the fluid and tumors
that can
at any moment
press and destroy
your ability

to see, to reason, to taste,
to walk, to breathe, to blink, to swallow

to hear, to feel, to speak, to laugh,
to be the person you recognize yourself to be

each block of nine
never more than
an arm's length away

is a measuring stick
an instant check up

no appointment needed
no need for a symptom
no need for a doctor

the 6's and 4's
2's and 7's all in their place

proving nothing
has changed in the past hour

this is your rabbit's foot
your meditation
your prayer
your worry stone

in the deep warm pocket
of that Chicago coat
bought
when your belly was still big
with your first son

another time
another life

The Cure

Hyperthermia Multi-cycle dose-intensive
Chemotherapy Photon Protocol Adjuvant
Immunotherapy Holding Hands Stem Cell
Transplants Radiation Chlorine Dioxide
Macaroni and Cheese Herceptin BX
Antitoxins Laughing Till You Cry Chi Gong
Brachytherapy Accelerated Partial Breast
Irradiation Reruns of Seinfeld Mastectomy
Cesium Chloride Meditation on Nuking
The Bad Cells Tuna Casserole Affirmations
on Loving The Bad Cells Temozolomide
Targeted Biologic Therapy Intensity-
modulated Radiation Vegan Diet A Five
Guys Cheeseburger Denritic Cell Therapy
Talking Your Boyfriend Into Having Sex
in Your Oncologist's Restroom Cyberknife
Hormone Therapy Dog Kisses Stereotactic
Radiosurgery Intravenous Vitamin C Oreo
Cookies The Velveteen Rabbit Lumpectomy
Tamoxifen Antineoplastons Yelling
GodDamnMotherfucker Photodynamic
Therapy Medical Marijuana Epigenetics
Napping With Your Sons Trastuzuma Chinese
Herbs Pulling Weeds Curcumin Spontaneous
Road Trip To Cape Canaveral Florida To Watch
The Last Space Shuttle Lift Off Ozone Therapy
Cesium Chloride Protocol Cat Licks Retinoic
Acid Ze Frank Stereotactic Radiosurgery Baking
Soda High RF Frequency Staying Up With
Your Sister All Night Like When You Were Five
Virotherapy Hyperbaric Oxygen Metabolic
Therapy David Bowie Juicing External Beam
Radiation DMSO Docetaxel Death

On The Edge

my writing teacher asked us
to use the phrase
on the edge

who the fuck is he kidding?

what I could say about *on the edge*
could fill encyclopedias

drown us in its downpour

fill the mouths of all the hungry

and make a sound
so piercing
so never ending
that nations would beg
to give up their weapons
to make it stop

on the edge?

I wrote the damn book.

Tolstoy and Proust wrote trifles
mere footnotes
to what I can say about
on the fuckin edge

six 800 page trilogies would be
the abbreviated introduction

let's start with cancer
not mine.

that would be easy

a piece of cake
walk in the park

No.

a daughter

in her prime
stretching into herself

basking like a sleek ocean liner
on the horizon of her world

terminal
they say

so
we wait

on the edge

that knife sharp
edge

that sliver of icy glacier
warming too fast

that raft heading down
the wrong rapids

and the unmistakable
rushing sound
a waterfall growing louder

as the shore slides past
in a blur
with nothing to grasp

on the edge?

Yeah.

I know that edge
I'm balancing my tea cup
on its thin porcelain rim

spreading my lunch
on its bare wire

The Fall

Sunday nights were mine

I picked you up in the afternoon
and we drove through
tree-lined neighborhoods
looking at porches and fences
to see what we could copy for your yard

we picked up tacos or Indian or Vietnamese
and headed home for the next round
of steroids, anti-seizure meds and
painkillers

we usually settled in to read or watch tv
propped up together in my bed
even though the guest room
had clean sheets and towels

the falling had begun in September
no tripping, no stumbling
only legs that disappeared
like a magic trick

now we're here
now we're not

your youngest son was always
first to your side
his long legs
only a few strides away

his arms grown strong
with devotion

whispering into your ear
it's ok mom. I got you

but that Sunday night
we went to the movies
maybe the fear of seizures was low
or the I-don't-care was high

I was game
and you were sure
screw the wheelchair
I'm walking

we crossed the street
in front of the theater
our arms intertwined
like stubborn vines

but this time
it was my ankle
that disappeared
bending just so

sending
me
then us
sprawling
in a wild collapse

a slow cascade
onto the popcorn-kernel
coke-splattered pavement

both of us
equally upended

our laughter rose
like a benediction
tears streaming

arms and legs tangled
each of us caught
in the sway and kick of the other
as if we were one body again

sobbing exhaustion
mouths open like weak birds
still laughing

throats upturned
to the executioner
foreheads wiped clean
for the oil

our eyes looking up
unmapped
unprepared
waiting for the first light of heaven

arms limp
ready to be raised

and in that split second
I found myself praying

please, can't you just
take us now?
like this
together?

Sunflowers

you arrived that afternoon
with arms full of
wild sunflowers
gathered by the roadside

their small yellow faces
turned this way and that
seven, eight flowers to each stem
searching for the sun

a silent echo
of the big-faced beauties
I grew by the front door
or the back fence
in every house
of your childhood

filling glass bottles
on our kitchen tables
roasting the seeds
with oil and salt
slippery snacks
in your small hands

we talked about being mothers
the breath-stopping wonder
unembarrassed love and
they-can-do-no-wrong pride

and your new worry
did I do a good enough job?

meanwhile the sunflowers
beamed their quiet approval
leaning forward
for the next story

the next burst of laughter
the next silken whisper

we didn't know this was
our last mother's day

that terminal had already
chosen a date

HOSPICE

Six Words

he does not look at us.

settling into the exam room sorting
a few pages in his folder

maybe he's still thinking about his
patient in Room B or a
research paper that has just arrived

he does not look at us.

he is a tall man fiercely
devoted to the lives of those
with the most aggressive breast cancer

he does not look at us.

but he sits on the swivel
stool and tells us the truth
his words
hang gently in the
antiseptic air

we have no more treatment options.

his eyes lift to meet yours.

the fluorescent light overhead stares
in innocent disbelief
the blinking monitor behind him
silently radios our distress

At Home

it was your wish to die at home
like your grandmother
your great grandmother and
all the women on your mother's side

no hospital
we promised

we would kidnap you
steal you away

to your bed
your home
your cats
your sons

the smell of earth and bayou
trees swaying in the wind
an afternoon shower
to wash clean your cottage
your land
wisteria climbing up the fence

so now
our promises kept
we sit by the open window

waiting

Sisters

your older sister drapes
your limp right arm
around her own neck

she waits
bent patiently
as your left arm slowly rises

your scarf covers the patchwork
light fuzz of dark hair and
bald spots

she whispers words against your
pale tender earlobe

That's it. Hold on to me.
I'm going to count to 3 and then I'll lift you.
Ok?

Hold on to me.

I got you.

1   2   3

feet planted

big sister
protector
heart-splayed warrior
scoops and lifts

overused muscles
tremble at the injustice

of losing you
this way

these are the hands
that steadied your bike at 5
cradled your broken arm at 6
found the right corset for Rocky Horror at 13

now they steady your wheelchair
on a sloping ramp
open prescription bottles
find the diapers that feel like real pants

I can hear your frothy giggles
on the back porch
as your steroid swollen body
drops into a chair

Now, stay put, ok?
I don't want to find you in that yard
pulling weeds.

and then your younger-sister response
halting
each carefully found word
a lilting
defiant tease

You are not. The boss. Of me.

The Boys

there always seems to be a
sweaty, smelly, voice-cracking
long-legged, shy, too loud
mumbling, joke-telling
boy

or two
or three
or four

on the sofa, on the porch, on the floor

in the refrigerator, in the spare bed
in the bathroom

leaning on
the counter
the table

two are yours
the sons you adore
without any stops
any hesitation

all in

your eyes alive
your hands on
their shoulders
their hair

dabbing clearasil
on a pimple

handing them
deodorant
along with
that look

the rest are
the almost-sons
come to talk
late at night
after school
on the weekends

your two boys
answer the late night
door knocks
throw extra blankets onto the couch
give up their chair on the porch
the one next to yours

why did she stop texting?
I thought she liked me

mom was drunk last night
and yelled at ME for smoking

school is 7 hours of boring hell

if I had a car I'd go to California
get wasted and
make millions being a hacker

you listen

your soft slanted smile
waiting for the moment
to explain

that girls don't wait 3 days for
you to text back

and parents will worry
even when they're drunk

and high school is boring
it just is
but you have to see it through

you remind them
that they are not
the father who doesn't come home
the brother who doesn't call

this is your life
you tell them
make something out of it
survive
fight
make it happen

this is the tribe of sons
who cried when your cancer came back
who sit by your hospice bed
holding your hand
talking softly into your stillness

telling you about the new girlfriend
the plan to return to college
the new used car

still wanting to make you proud

you taught them
how to live

and in the end
you are teaching them
how to die

The Mission

we are a squad of four
working in12 hours shifts

sister, boyfriend
mother, adopted dad

standing watch
measuring pain-killers
with military precision
watching for landmines, snipers
and rogue fires

2 of us on day shift
2 on night shift
meeting to debrief in the middle

tea becomes coffee
granola gives way to candy bars
hamburgers and fries
chicken fried steaks
and then

our throats close
unable to swallow
dry
parched

absent of appetite
filled only with the sound of
your guttural breath

and the hope of having
one more hour
a few more minutes

another dawn
            with you

The Call

They all come
as if they know
today
is your last day

you lay
on your side
curled as if napping
on the broad chest of Morpheus
your favorite scarf is wrapped
around your head to stave off a chill

the hospital bed is in the living room
by the bright open windows
two young squirrels chase
each other
up a nearby tree

your best friend since high school
driver on road trips
keeper of teenage secrets
maid of honor
and second mother to your boys
holds your hand silently
listening
for one last word

your ex-husband
stops pacing
finally resting his head
by your pillow
speaking to you

one last time
of the sons you share

the friend who joined you
for toddler days in the park
together raising
your babies into grown ups
comes every day now
bringing coffee and chocolate

one son brings his new girlfriend
to meet you
she takes my hand and tells me
her grandfather was in hospice last month

your other son takes his place
by your side
and holds your hand
his girlfriend already like a daughter
holds your other

your sister brings out
the baby albums
and the boys tease each other
about chubby cheeks and bad haircuts

the almost-sons come too

friends from Chicago
serenade you on borrowed guitars

friends from Austin
bring their daughters

calls ring from New York
Tennessee and Florida
California and Iowa
far flung places where those
you have loved
are loving back

there is pizza and smoking outside
barbecue and sweet tea
sushi and chai

there is laughter in the kitchen
stories on the back porch
cuttings from your plants to take home

your breath is loud, steady and strong
your heart still unwilling to let go

a slow radiance builds in your face
as swelling diminishes and you move
further way from us
closer to a world
where we cannot follow

you
at the center
with life swirling around you
someone always by your side
telling you their secrets

somehow
        you sent out the call

the door is open
my bags are packed
and soon
I'll be on my way

He was usually the one you called when you had a scheme, a wild dream, a secret, a worry, a fear. He listened between the words, behind and beneath the syllables. When you were diagnosed, he was your first call from the doctor's office.

It's not a swollen lymph. It's cancer, you told him. *How do I tell Mom? How much do I tell the boys?*

He told you to simply meet me at home, sit me down and tell me. He told you to trust me, that we would hold this, go through this together. From then on he answered your calls on the first ring, no matter where he was or what he was doing. He was your anchor. The one you didn't have to protect. He was your friend, my partner, your adopted Dad. Each month he boarded cars and airplanes to be with you. With us. Walking in step, by your side and mine.

He wrapped Santa gifts into the dark mornings each Christmas Eve for 13 years. Lego toys to books on physics, Barbie dolls to steampunk boots, Dr Seuss to The Hunger Games. He lit fires under your writing, guided your editing and paid the tuition to your first writers conference. When a second round of full brain radiation gave us the chance of a couple of more months with you, he cut his hair into a mohawk that matched your own.

There were no short conversations between you, no topic untouched - poetry and politics, motherhood and mother earth, cancer and death and what you would miss when you were gone. He listened.

And, finally, it was his hands that held your head in the darkened room as your last breath escaped your body. The four of us, mother, sister, boyfriend and adopted father, were trying not to hover by your side that night. We felt your readiness to leave and imagined it might be too hard for you to go in the presence of those you loved. As he walked through your room, he felt a call to place his hands gently beneath your head. Maybe to help carry the weight of that final decision. To ease your last burden. He told us that you took one breath. And then one more. And then you were gone.

The room was strangely quiet. He stayed with you. Listening. Until he was sure. And then he came to gather us into this new silence, this world absent of you, so we could tend to your body and cry, open windows and doors to the night air. Letting you go.

It was right that he was with you. You were his daughter, as truly as if he had conceived you. He was your Dad. And although he was not there to catch your damp, small body on the day you entered the world, it was his hands that cradled you as you left it.

AFTER

In Beauty: May 7th, 2014

2:32am

all night
we had stood guard
counting medications
arguing, holding one another
crying
laughing
without another
24 hours between us

we circle your bed
exhausted
not talking
not touching

the room is bathed
in silence so deep
our ears
our lashes
our fingertips
vibrate
ring
ache

for the last 72 hours
your wet
guttural breathing has been
our constant companion

now
there is
silence

the air
the walls
the sheets
the floor under
our feet

still

unoccupied
vacant

leaving behind
your curled pale body
under the white
down comforter

at peace

dreaming into the answers
we have long forgotten

a hawk lifting
into the dark morning sky
heading for the waning moon

into the day just dawning
past the horizon
beyond our view

wings outstretched
each feather a rudder
guiding your journey home

diving into each current
testing the flow
the down of your throat
exposed and proud

unafraid
unafraid

2:54am

we raise our eyes
and as one
we leave your bedside
and begin
sweeping up syringes and lotions
prescriptions and patches
bed pads and eye drops

trash bags are filled
carried out
in our eagerness to dispose of
illness and pain

fresh sheets
clean soft pajamas
washcloths
warm water and soap

we open doors and windows
and a wind picks up

you sweep through
light as a kiss

whispering
care for
one another

3:25am

your body
prone and elegant
washed
still warm
dry lips
moist and soft

you glow with a light
we have watched
increase by the day
by the hour

the steroid weight is gone
now there is only
the young mother
the vibrant
alive woman
lover of the pen
the page
the fight for justice
the wry twist of humor

that woman
lies in beauty
in herself
in her forever-ness

as we stumble to find
our feet
in a world
forever
changed

Your Memorial

you wanted a place
open as the sky

you were done with suffering
so I promised you a church with no cross

free of symbols
enough space to hear

one's own voice
yours

or whoever might speak
to our still and reverent hearts

we chose this place
because of the windows

because of the light
because of the holy blue sky

our friends, our family
entered one or two at a time

threads of connection
drawing them to this place

some traveled 1000 miles
30 years, 5 jobs ago

how eloquently your sister
spoke of you

I have not lost my sister.
Time and space do not separate us.

They do not separate you from her.
We are simply rearranged and poised for the next
adventure.

and your eldest son

She taught us how to listen and how to hold things dear.
That questioning authority is an obligation and
birthday cake for breakfast is simply part of the
celebration.

he quoted Marquez
your niece read Neruda

and finally
after eulogies and music and photographs
before we feasted on your favorite cookies

we ended with your voice
your words
to stem our bleeding hearts

If I could speak in another language
I would tell you that today
only the immediacy of bravery and forgiveness
is required.

Avoiding Lentils

I once asked
if you wanted to learn
to make lentil soup
and you looked at me

chin tucked in, head askew
your brows knitted
half laughing
and why would I do that?

you had an irrevocable certainty
that my hands would always be here
to produce a lifetime
of warm, earthy lentil soup
every fall and winter
year after year

and I smiled
because you were right

these hands
would have gladly delivered bowls
glass containers
of brown lentils
soaked and simmered
with rich tomato sauce and spices
bits of chicken or sausage
onion and celery
spinach and carrots
ready to be ladled over
jasmine rice

I would have fed you
to the end of your days

and I did

but today when I open my pantry
I see the bag
split
spilled across the dark floor
tiny brown circles
hard and uncooked

Unswept.
Untended.

each one a small world
where you are not

He Can't Leave the House

he calls for take out

can't bear to be away
from your scent
lingering still
in the sage folds
of your bedroom curtains

the hint of fabric softener
in your body pillow
the earthy cinnamon of your pores

he doesn't run the AC
even now
with the Texas summer
full upon us

the heat
the searing hot glove
of ice
gripping his chest
is a welcome distraction

he walks the rooms
of your small cottage
telling you
how the dishes are finally washed
how the cat sits by his chair
both of them listening

for you

in the shower
your spoon in the cereal bowl
the creak of your bed

he tells you
about the seed he planted
in the terra cotta pot
on the front porch
sitting now
in the sun

3 inches tall
in its young green glory
its tiny fragile leaves
unfurling
each one a promise

he's given it your name
and searches the internet
again
for how
to keep you alive

until you bud and bloom
and he can
inhale you
into the empty cavern
of his broken heart

Misunderstanding

I keep expecting you to
walk in the door

What?
Really?
You thought I was dead?

In the Blink of an Eye

We are both propped up in my bed reading.
You take the Eben Alexander book off my
nightstand and get lost in its pages for two
hours. Then you turn to me and say, *Did you
read about all this wandering in the darkness
after he's brain dead?*

Yes, I reply. Silence. You set your eyes deep
into the text again. A moment later I hear the
book close sharply and you hand it to me, to
be returned to the nightstand where you found
it. Your other hand reaches for the manuscript
you are editing for work. Your voice is sure,
almost insulted. *I will not be wandering in the
darkness.*

I smile, remembering my mother, your
grandmother, 90 years old, in the ER after a
6 hour wait. Rising elegantly, reaching for her
cane she announced, *There will be no dying
tonight.* Then she headed for the door, damn
her heart palpitations, her shortness of breath.
She was going home, by cab or in my car, and
which one didn't matter.

Two months after your death a medium
tells me, *She wants you to know that she was
wrapped in love here and in the blink of an
eye, she was wrapped in love there. She wants
you to know there was no wandering in the
darkness.*

The Skydiver

the photo was taken
after the nylon dome
filled and gently
deposited you to the earth

after your wild, free
take-me-lord leap

falling
arms outstretched
reaching into
those long
slow motion moments

free and flying
with only a fickle wind
keeping you afloat

the world
wide and open
the curve of the earth
the houses
streets

lives below
scattered across the green

before the pull of gravity
insisted you come down

on the ground
arms full of yards and yards
of parachute
your familiar long-legged stride

your head still full
of the rushing wind
your un-bound smile

the same smile you wore at
6 months
4 years
8 years
before caution
before secrets
before the lines of joy
became entangled

you returned to the sky
again and again

and in those long moments
of falling
you were making yourself
ready
for the real risk
the real ride

allowing that same wind
to rip away the fear
of having children
you could not protect
the marriage that might not last forever

filling both hands
with yards and yards of living

three months before you died
you asked all of us to jump with you

one sister, two parents, one best friend,
a boyfriend and two precious sons

but we couldn't

couldn't place one more person we loved
into the greedy hands of fate

already we were trying
to prepare ourselves for your next flight

packing the chute
studying the weather
preparing to pull the cord
to release you
at just the right moment

today I bend to this grief
companion of my days
the future
a toy village
too far away to see

and then I hear your voice
clear and demanding

Leap!

Pull open the heavy door
step out into the thin air
the wind will carry you down
I am here
I will catch you.

If I Could Speak Another Language
by Tina Borja

I have this idea that if I could speak another language
I could tell you everything

I could tell you
about the avocado and sprout sandwiches on whole wheat
that I took to school in first grade
and how my grandmother ate fresh artichokes
with pitted black olives from the can
on toothpick swords for dinner sometimes

In another language
without you wondering
what this has to do with you
I could tell you how
when forced to shop
I run my fingers along the rack
until I touch something soft enough
to be worth seeing

How I hate trying things on
because as young and thin
as I imagine myself to be
rude awakenings are not to be had in public

How I have always preferred men's clothing
how it helps me when I want to be invisible

I could tell you that sometimes
when I wake up in the night
it is not because of the train
but because of my dreams

That turning the pillow to the cool side
used to make things right again

But today I am tucked into that place
where my whole body
is resentfully along for the ride
the what-if journey of the brain
that resembles sleep
but is not

This I know

If I could speak another language
I could kiss with plentiful abandon
those kisses that make even movie stars
believe they are in love again

If I wanted to
I could dress in ridiculous
bright, tight, sheer or all-the-above clothing
accessorized with a canary yellow chiffon scarf
and dark sunglasses

I would have the courage to create
big, loud, messy art at random
and in abundance

I could tell you that, like my son,
he at four and me at six
I too wondered what came after the sky
how at ten
my fingers played the piano

but I didn't
and still can't

That I am superstitious
not in that baseball-player-obsessive-compulsive way
but in that if-you-say-it-out-loud-it-is-true way

I could explain to you quite scientifically
how words spoken out loud
break into a million pieces
exiting our bodies
and entering the air all around us forever

Forever available to recollect
reconstruct and replay

Forever available to re-live
or, if you believe in it, regret

I can also definitely tell you
that I don't believe in regret
in the same way that I don't believe
in feeling guilty
in the way I don't give in to fear

I still have difficulty remembering
what made me angry or hurt

If I could speak another language
I could explain that
ever searching for the few loopholes

we have been given
I choose to believe that writing it down
is not the same as saying it out loud

That writing it down
makes whatever you have written
possibly fiction
and not subject to coming true

I know that these words
spoken in another language won't
cause you to think I am crazy

In another language
I could tell you I believe
my once diagnosed dissociative disorder
is why I hear with the utmost clarity
conversations real
and imagined
and dead people speak

That this happens most often
when pulling weeds, pruning bushes
painting and driving

That for this reason
I prefer these chores in surround-sound silence
except for the driving
where I find music an essential force
to keep body and mind on task
and talkative spirits distracted

If I could be absolutely certain
you would not understand me
I could reassure you
that my wrist was broken that June
not by pulling potato vines
from the fence in a thunderstorm
but rather by a conspiracy of angels
in a last ditch effort to make me listen

If you heard it in another language
familiar syllables in disorder
you would believe me when I told you
that my hands can heal illness
brought to our bodies by fear and misgivings
and that I could breathe underwater
were it not for this one last vestige of doubt

I could tell you how at five
I almost suffocated on my understanding of God
that I believed, as I was told
that God was quite literally all around us
which to me
meant he filled the air with invisible
yet palpable God-stuff

That as I took my first breath
upon learning this
I felt I would choke
and spent the rest of that night
beneath my sister
in her bunk and my fish mobile

meticulously sifting God-air
through my clenched teeth
so I would not swallow
so large a piece of God-chunk
as to hurt myself or him

I did this until I fell asleep
mesmerized by the fish
hyperventilated
and exhausted from my efforts
to keep us both alive
and in recognizable form

In another language
I would tell you
that the knowledge of my own irrelevance
runs concurrent to the freedom
of my unlimited potential

And when I want it to
liberates my mind and my body
to be as extraordinary as my spirit

If I could speak in another language
I would tell you
that bad things
don't happen to bad people
that bad things happen
and some people just don't believe
they are bad things

And I would tell you that today

only the immediacy of bravery and forgiveness
is required

If I could speak in another language
I would tell you
that I avoid rooftops
not for a fear of falling
but for a fear of jumping
because along
with the perfect inconsequence
of my life
comes too
my belief in the perfect inconsequence
of my death

I might even start telling you
that I have died a thousand times over

but that is a long conversation
for another night.

Acknowledgments

This book would not have been conceived without the generous and unselfish support of three writing communities – the Spectrum Center Writer's Guild in Houston, Texas, the Hollowdeck Press Writer's Guild at the Firedrake Center for the Arts in Maryland, and the annual Hollowdeck Press June Projects Retreat in Boulder, Colorado.

Each of these communities was created and continues to be artfully tended by Max Regan, a skilled writing teacher and developmental editor. With a deft hand he leads us to find our own unique writing voices and then holds us firmly while we thrash about, insisting every word we write is precious until we give up and begin to edit for craft, clarity and meaning.

I am forever grateful that when I was frozen with shock at my daughter's diagnosis, Max simply turned me toward poetry. He told me that I could say more with less in poetry, that it would allow me to finish a small piece and rest. He told me that if I stopped writing, Tina would probably kill us both. So I wrote. And while I wrote, my fellow writers in these three communities listened, held my grief and my rage, gave me feedback and kept me going.

First, I want to thank my monthly Staying Serious group – Barbara Carle, Melanie Miller, Ellen Seaton, Diana Galindo, Kirsten Cerre and Ron Bueker. You have been my mainstays, holding me firmly on my path month after month until I could see a collection rather than random poems.

In the Maryland community, Susan Gordon, Jennifer Dove-Robinson, Maggie Babb, Anita Rosenberg, Moo Briddell, Marilyn Williams and Marcia Davies have been my cheerleaders. You brought me solace through flowers and cards, reminding me that the beauty of the natural world can heal and give comfort.

A huge thank you to the returning writer warriors of the annual Hollowdeck Press June Projects Retreat - Ann Loar Brooks, Shireen Day, Signe Hovem, Dorothy Van Soest, Roger Roffman, Mary Randall, Sindee Ernst, and Bonnie Aona. You have been witnesses to my process, evaluated my work with a critical eye and an open heart.

I want to additionally acknowledge the generosity of my peer editors who took the time to carefully critique my last draft with such skilled attention - Barbara Carle, Devi Records, Ann Loar Brooks, Jennifer Dove-Robinson, Susanna Barlow and Shireen Day. I couldn't have seen the manuscript clearly without you. You brought me home.

Thank you to my colleagues who watched over Spectrum Center when I needed to be with Tina or just be alone, especially Suzan Cotellesse, Marilyn Denham, Helen Racz and Monica Mullen. Your steady support and love still lives in my heart. I am also grateful to the attendees, teachers and wellness practitioners who donated their time and talents to our fundraisers, as well as everyone who sent in donations when we were tackling bills not covered by insurance or salaries.

To those friends who read my first attempts and through these years turned me back to the page when I was hurting the most - Joleen Bishop, Bob Erwin, Sr. Kim Marie Jordan, Chris Murphy, Christin Staszesky Harper, Satya Shepherd, Sandra Nicholas, Sita Lewi, Crosby Bean, Lynn Sellers and Henry Morrow. Your encouragement and steady friendship mattered.

Words cannot express my admiration and love for the beautiful Elaine Brewer and her team at the Rice University technology department who obtained approval and stayed late on a Friday night to print Tina's children's book in full four-color press. Because of you, Tina could hold her book in her hands while she was still fully conscious four days before her death. She could no longer speak, but her smile said it all.

My eternal appreciation goes to the Rice University professors who, after metastasis, helped make up the difference between Tina's short-term disability and her salary. Most of all, I am grateful to you for continuing to believe in Tina by giving her the editing work she loved to do for as long as her brain allowed. And a special thank you to Pershant Kale for his gracious generosity to Tina's sons.

My daughter, Teresa, who is also a writer and poet, has become the steady core of our family; the one we lean into when the road becomes uncertain. You believe in me at every turn and pick up the fallen pieces. I admire you and love you. I hope I have adequately expressed your heart, your bravery and your devotion to your younger sister in these pages.

Last, I want to express my abiding love for my family who walked this path with me – my grandchildren, Abby, Nika, Jack, Gabe and Anna Rose; the boys' Aunt Sheri; my sister, Ximena; my son-in-law Larry; my adopted daughter, Anna; and of course, Ozzie. Each of you loved Tina, fought for her, and kept the pieces of me glued together. Tina's spirit will continue to shine through all our lives. I look forward to seeing what she makes of us.

Rosa Glenn Reilly is a poet, writer and the Founder and Director of Spectrum Center in Houston, TX. Founded in 1988, Spectrum Center is Houston's longest standing holistic wellness center, offering traditional as well as non-traditional approaches to health and personal growth. Rosa enjoys a successful counseling practice working with individuals and couples in the areas of adult development, life transition, intimacy, crisis, trauma resolution and grief. Born in Santiago Chile, she comes from a long lineage of writers, artists, healers and activists, traditions that have been passed down to all the members of her family.

www.rosaglennreilly.com